Scripture POWER!

ISBN 13: 978-1-4621-1638-6

Published by CFI, an imprint of Cedar Fort, Inc.
2373 W. 700 S., Springville, UT 84663
Distributed by Cedar Fort, Inc., www.cedarfort.com

LIBRARY OF CONGRESS CATALOGING-IN-PUBLICATION DATA

Dorathy, Elizabeth, 1974- author.
Scripture power! : Book of Mormon journal for children / Elizabeth Dorathy.
     pages cm
Encourages children to read the Book of Mormon daily and keep a spiritual journal.
Includes bibliographical references and index.
ISBN 978-1-4621-1638-6 (layflat binding : alk. paper)
1. Book of Mormon--Study and teaching. 2. Mormon children--Conduct of life. 3. Mormon children--Spiritual life. 4. Diaries--Authorship. I. Title.

BX8627.D66 2015
289.3'22--dc23

                                  2015021013

Cover design by Shawnda T. Craig
Cover design © 2015 Lyle Mortimer
Edited and typeset by Jessica B. Ellingson

Printed in the United States of America

10 9 8 7 6 5 4 3 2 1

Printed on acid-free paper

Scripture POWER!

Book of Mormon Journal for Children

Elizabeth Dorathy

CFI
an imprint of Cedar Fort, Inc.
Springville, UT

Note

Some of the journal activities fulfill requirements for your Faith in God Award. As you go through the journal, you will see little symbols. This means that doing this activity will also fulfill a Faith in God requirement. The letters inside the symbol correspond with the different headings in your Faith in God guidebook as follows.

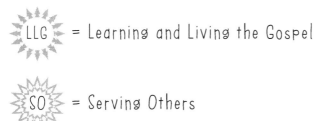

LLG = Learning and Living the Gospel

SO = Serving Others

DT = Developing Talents

1 Nephi 1:1–3

Nephi says he was born "of goodly parents." What do you think that means?

_____

_____

_____

_____

1 Nephi 2:1–4

Lehi does everything the Lord asks him to. He is obedient. What does it mean to be obedient?

_____

_____

_____

_____

1 Nephi 3:4-7

To *murmur* means to complain. Laman and Lemuel complain because the job they were given was hard. Nephi knows it is a hard job, but he knows the Lord will help him. When you have something hard to do, do you complain or ask for help? What is something hard you have done?

_____

_____

_____

_____

1 Nephi 4:1-3

Nephi has faith that the Lord will help them if they are obedient. His brothers are still complaining. If you were with Nephi, what would you do?

_____

_____

_____

_____

1 Nephi 5:1-6

Nephi's mother is upset and worried about her sons. She starts complaining and stops having faith. Sometimes when we are upset, it's hard to be obedient, and we start to complain. Her husband, Lehi, helped her to calm down. How do you calm down when you are upset?

_____

_____

_____

_____

1 Nephi 6:4-6

Nephi says that everyone who helped write the Book of Mormon only wrote things "of worth" to us who read it. What do you think "of worth" means?

_____

_____

_____

_____

1 Nephi 7:8, 16—18

Laman and Lemuel are angry with Nephi and tie him up. What does Nephi do?

_____

_____

_____

_____

1 Nephi 8:2, 5—12

This is called "Lehi's dream." When Lehi eats the fruit, he feels "great joy." When he feels that joy, who does he want to share it with?

_____

_____

_____

_____

1 Nephi 8:13–18

In the dream, who in Lehi's family comes to eat the fruit? Who doesn't?

_____

_____

_____

_____

1 Nephi 8:19–21, 23–24

In the dream, Lehi sees large groups of people trying to get to the tree to eat the fruit. Is it easy or hard to get to the tree? What makes it hard?

_____

_____

_____

_____

1 Nephi 8:26-28

In the dream, there is a building full of people making fun of those who are trying to get to the tree. What would you do if someone made fun of you for doing what is right?

_____

_____

_____

_____

1 Nephi 11:1-5, 10-11, 25

Nephi asks to see the same dream his father, Lehi, saw. Sometimes dreams mean something special. In Lehi's dream, everything is a symbol of something else. Nephi wants to know what each thing means. An angel shows him. What does the rod of iron represent? What does the tree represent?

_____

_____

_____

1 Nephi 12:17—18

In the dream, what do the mists of darkness represent? What do you think that means?

_____

_____

_____

_____

1 Nephi 13:19—23

This is still Nephi's vision. The angel is showing Nephi the future. He shows him a book that is of "great worth." What book do you think that is?

_____

_____

_____

_____

1 Nephi 14:5—7

The angel tells Nephi that people need to repent. What does it mean to repent?

_____

_____

_____

_____

1 Nephi 15:1—3, 6—11

After his vision, Nephi talks to his brothers. They are confused about the dream their father, Lehi, told them about. What does Nephi tell them to do when they have questions?

_____

_____

_____

_____

1 Nephi 16:17–18, 20, 23–24, 31

Nephi's bow breaks, and he can't hunt for food. His family starts to complain, but Nephi tries to solve the problem. When things don't go the way you expect, what can you do to try to solve the problem?

_____

_____

_____

1 Nephi 17:7–10

DT

The Lord tells Nephi to build a ship. Nephi doesn't know how, so he asks the Lord to help him. Does the Lord help him? Has someone ever helped you learn something new? How does learning new talents and improving the talents you have help you to serve Heavenly Father and others?

_____

_____

_____

_____

1 Nephi 18:9–13, 20–23

Laman and Lemuel are still making bad choices. This time they are using rude words. Why does the Lord care about the words we say?

_____

_____

_____

_____

1 Nephi 19:1–3

Nephi makes plates out of metal. These are not plates to eat from; they are thin pieces of metal to write on. Some of those writings are in the Book of Mormon. Why do you think Heavenly Father wanted Nephi to write on metal plates?

_____

_____

_____

_____

1 Nephi 20:1–2

Do you remember when the Lord commanded Lehi to leave his home in Jerusalem because the people were becoming wicked? The Lord is talking to those people. They call themselves God's people, but they do not follow His commandments. Have you ever promised you would do something but didn't do it? When you do what you promise you will do, how do you feel?

_____

_____

_____

_____

1 Nephi 21:8–11

These verses are talking about how Jesus helps us. What is one way He helps you?

_____

_____

_____

_____

1 Nephi 22:1–2

The Spirit is also called the Holy Ghost. The prophet knows everything we need to know because the Spirit tells him. Who is the prophet today?

_____

_____

_____

_____

2 Nephi 1:1, 4–6

A covenant is a two-way promise. The Lord promises He will lead Lehi's family to a new land if Lehi does his part by obeying the Lord. What promises has Heavenly Father given you?

_____

_____

_____

_____

2 Nephi 2:6-7

Jesus suffered and died so that when we make mistakes we can be forgiven and still return to live with Heavenly Father. We need to have a "broken heart" and a "contrite spirit." This means we need to feel sorry for our wrong choice and want to be better. Have you ever made a wrong choice? How did you make it better or fix it?

_____

_____

_____

_____

_____

_____

_____

_____

2 Nephi 3:7-9

A seer is a prophet. This is talking about Joseph Smith. Who is Joseph Smith? Read about Joseph Smith's First Vision in Joseph Smith—History 1:10-20. Give a lesson on Joseph Smith's First Vision in family home evening. What is one thing you learned about Joseph Smith?

_____

_____

_____

_____

2 Nephi 4:5-7

Lehi blesses his children before he dies. Have you ever had a priesthood blessing? If so, write about it:

_____

_____

_____

_____

Nephi and the people who want to obey the Lord leave Laman and Lemuel and the group who doesn't want to obey the Lord. Nephi's people are called Nephites. The other people are called Lamanites. The Nephites build a temple. How does the temple bless you and your family?

_____

_____

_____

_____

2 Nephi 6:1–2

Jacob is Nephi's brother. He is given the priesthood. The priesthood is the power and the authority to act for God. Who do you know who has the priesthood?

_____

_____

_____

_____

2 Nephi 7:4-5

These are the words of a prophet named Isaiah, who we read about in the Bible. Jacob is reading his words to the Nephites. Isaiah says that God helps him to say the right things. God also helps him to learn what he needs to know. Can Heavenly Father help you learn? What can you do to have Heavenly Father's help with your learning?

_____

_____

_____

2 Nephi 8:12

When we are afraid, Jesus comforts us. When you are scared, what do you do to feel better? Write about a time you were scared and Jesus helped you feel better.

_____

_____

_____

_____

2 Nephi 9:23

All people must be baptized. Have you been baptized?
If so, write about how you felt on your baptism day.
If you haven't been baptized yet, write about how you
can prepare for your baptism.

_____

_____

_____

_____

2 Nephi 10:23–24

LLG

Every day, you can make right choices. How has making
right choices helped you have more faith?

_____

_____

_____

_____

2 Nephi 11:1-2, 4-6, 8

Nephi says his "soul delighteth" in Isaiah's words and teaching people about Christ. This means these things make him very happy. What are some things your "soul delighteth" in?

---

2 Nephi 12:2-3

Nephi is still writing words from the prophet Isaiah. The house they are writing about is the temple. Have you ever been to a temple? What was it like?

---

2 Nephi 14:5–6

The Lord will always protect us and give us a "place of refuge." This is a special place where we feel safe. Where is a place you feel happy and safe?

_____

_____

_____

_____

2 Nephi 16:1, 8

Isaiah has a vision where he sees the Lord. The Lord asks if someone will do some work for Him, and Isaiah volunteers. Write about a time you volunteered for a hard job.

_____

_____

_____

_____

2 Nephi 18:11-12

Sometimes, following Heavenly Father's commandments means doing something different from what everyone else is doing. What is one thing that is hard to do when other people are doing something different?

_____

_____

_____

_____

2 Nephi 19:6

This verse is talking about Jesus. Jesus has a lot of names. One of His names is "Wonderful." What are some of the names or things people call you? What are some words that describe you?

_____

_____

_____

_____

2 Nephi 20:1–2

SO

Jesus wants us to love and help the people around us with the things they need. Write down a plan to help your neighbor or a member of your family and then do it.

_____

_____

_____

_____

2 Nephi 22:1–6

LLG

These verses are a testimony of Jesus. A testimony is what you know or believe to be true. Write down your testimony of Jesus Christ.

_____

_____

_____

_____

2 Nephi 24:7-8

Someday Jesus will come back and everything will be peaceful. These verses say everyone will sing. What do you think that will be like? What is your favorite Primary song to sing?

_____

_____

_____

2 Nephi 25:23, 26

We try to make right choices, but sometimes we make mistakes. Even when we make mistakes, Jesus and Heavenly Father still love us. Because of Jesus, we can be forgiven for our mistakes and live with Him again someday. Write about a time when someone forgave you when you made a mistake.

_____

_____

_____

_____

2 Nephi 26:29—30

The Lord says that we should not love ourselves more than other people. We should love other people the way Heavenly Father loves them. This is sometimes hard and takes some practice. Who is sometimes hard for you to love? What can you do this week to show that person love?

_____

_____

_____

_____

_____

_____

_____

_____

2 Nephi 27:6–7, 11

The book this talks about is the Book of Mormon. After it was written, it was sealed and buried. Hundreds of years later, Moroni visited Joseph Smith as an angel and told him where to find the plates it was written on. Joseph translated and published the book, and now everyone can read the words of these prophets from long ago. How do you feel about the Book of Mormon?

_____

_____

_____

_____

_____

_____

_____

_____

2 Nephi 29:7–8

The world is a big place with a lot of people in it. Heavenly Father knows and loves each person. The Book of Mormon is the writings of one group of people who lived a long time ago in one area of the world. The Bible is the writings of a group of people who lived in a different area of the world. Both books teach and testify of Jesus Christ. What is your favorite scripture story? Is it from the Book of Mormon or from the Bible?

_____

_____

_____

_____

_____

_____

_____

_____

2 Nephi 30:12–13

When Jesus comes again, there will be peace. Even the animals won't want to harm each other. What is your favorite animal? Why?

_____

_____

_____

_____

2 Nephi 31:4–7

The Lamb of God is another name for Jesus. This is about Jesus being baptized. Why was Jesus baptized?

_____

_____

_____

_____

2 Nephi 32:3–5

Sometimes when the scriptures use the word *knock*, it means "pray." If you don't understand something in the scriptures, what should you do?

_____

_____

_____

_____

2 Nephi 33:3–4

Nephi loves his people so much that he prays for them and cries because of their wrong choices. Who do you think prays for you? Who can you pray for?

_____

_____

_____

_____

Jacob 1:7

To labor diligently means to work hard. They worked hard as missionaries. Write letters to missionaries you know and thank them for their hard work. What can you do now to prepare for a mission?

_____

_____

_____

_____

Jacob 2:12–14, 17–18

Jacob tells his people that they have been blessed with riches, but some of the people have started thinking they are better than others who aren't as rich. This is called pride. What does Jacob say they should do?

_____

_____

_____

_____

Jacob 3:1–2

What do you think it means to be "pure in heart"?

_____

_____

_____

_____

Jacob 4:1–3

Jacob says he can only write the most important things because it is hard to carve his words into the plates. He says he does it for his family. Have you ever done something hard for someone else?

_____

_____

_____

_____

Jacob 5:1–3

Jacob writes the words of a different prophet named Zenos. Zenos starts to tell a story about an olive tree. The olive tree is a symbol of the people of Israel. This kind of story is called a parable. Do you know any parables?

_____

_____

_____

Jacob 6:4–5

"Stiffnecked" means stubborn. This verse says that Heavenly Father loves His children no matter what and always wants to help them, even when they are being stubborn and making wrong choices. When someone in your family is being stubborn, what can you do to show them you still love them?

_____

_____

_____

Jacob 7:24-25

The Lamanites hate the Nephites and keep starting wars with them. What do the Nephites do to protect themselves?

_____

_____

_____

_____

Enos 1:1-5

LLG

Enos is Jacob's son. He prays for an entire day and into the night. What is the longest you have prayed? How does prayer protect you and help you stay close to Heavenly Father and Jesus?

_____

_____

_____

_____

31

Jarom 1:11–12

Jarom is Enos's son. His people are starting to make bad choices. The prophets tell them over and over again to make good choices. They need a lot of reminders. What is something your parents remind you over and over again to do?

_____

_____

_____

Omni 1:12, 23, 25

This book is a collection of writings from five different people who each wrote a little. Amaleki writes about a prophet named Mosiah and Mosiah's son Benjamin. Amaleki is the great-great-grandson of Jarom. Do you know the name of your great-great-grandfather? Ask someone to help you make a pedigree chart, with the names of your parents and grandparents.

_____

_____

_____

Words of Mormon 1:13, 17–18

Mormon is a prophet who lives later. Toward the end of the Book of Mormon, he has all of the plates and he is putting them all together. Here he has added some of his writings about King Benjamin. He says King Benjamin was a "holy man." What do you think that means?

_____

_____

_____

_____

Mosiah 1:1–3

King Benjamin teaches his sons many things, including an ancient language and the gospel. What are some things your family teaches you?

_____

_____

_____

_____

Mosiah 2:1–2, 5–7

King Benjamin wanted to talk to all of his people. He stood on a tower, and each family turned their tents so they could listen to him. How does the prophet speak to all of us today? Read a recent talk given by the prophet at conference. What can you do to follow the prophet?

_____

_____

_____

_____

Mosiah 3:1, 5–11

King Benjamin is teaching his people about Jesus Christ. What did you learn about Jesus from these verses?

_____

_____

_____

_____

Mosiah 4:9–10

Do you believe in God? Who is He? What are some words that describe Him?

Mosiah 5:15

DT

"Good works" are nice things you do for others. List five good works you can do to help around your home.

Mosiah 6:3–5

How old was Mosiah when he became king? How old are you?

_____

_____

_____

_____

Mosiah 7:1–3

Many years before, a group of people left Mosiah's area (called Zarahemla) and traveled to another place called the land of Lehi-Nephi. Mosiah sends a group of men to check on them. Have you ever gone on a trip to visit a different place? Where did you go, and what did you do there?

_____

_____

_____

_____

Mosiah 8:1–3

Ammon and the men who go to Lehi-Nephi meet the king, who tells them the history of their people since leaving Zarahemla. What is the king's name?

_____

_____

_____

_____

Mosiah 9:6–10

This is the writing of Zeniff, who brought the first group of people from Zarahemla to Lehi-Nephi. We are jumping back in time to when they first arrive and rebuild the city of Lehi-Nephi and start growing food. Have you ever had a garden or grown a plant that gave you food? What is your favorite fruit or vegetable?

_____

_____

_____

_____

The Lamanites start to attack the people of Zeniff. The Lamanites are descendants of Laman and Lemuel. These verses tell us that Laman and Lemuel were mad at Lehi, their father, for making them leave Jerusalem and at Nephi for being their leader. Because of this, they taught their kids and all the following generations to hate the kids and descendants of Nephi (they are called the Nephites). This is called a grudge. A grudge is when you feel angry, and instead of forgiving someone, you stay mad for a long time. Have you ever felt angry at someone? Did you forgive them? How did you feel?

_____

_____

_____

_____

_____

_____

Mosiah 11:1, 3

Noah becomes king. He is wicked. He taxes his people more than what is needed. A tax is when you take part of what others earn. How do you think Noah's people felt?

_____

_____

_____

_____

Mosiah 12:1, 9, 17

The Lord sends Abinadi, a prophet, to tell King Noah and his people that they are making wrong choices and need to repent. How do they feel when they hear Abinadi? What do they do to him?

_____

_____

_____

_____

Mosiah 13:1–3, 5

King Noah asks to speak with Abinadi. Abinadi starts to preach to the king. The king's men try to grab Abinadi, but Abinadi is protected by the Lord. What does it say Abinadi looked like?

_____

_____

_____

_____

Mosiah 15:1–2

Who does Abinadi teach them about?

_____

_____

_____

_____

Mosiah 16:9

Abinadi compares Jesus Christ to a light. How does he say Jesus is like a light?

_____

_____

_____

_____

Mosiah 17:1–4

One of king Noah's men believes the words of Abinadi. What is his name?

_____

_____

_____

_____

Mosiah 18:1, 3, 35

Alma starts to preach in secret, and many people believe his words and are baptized. How many people follow Alma?

_____

_____

_____

_____

Mosiah 19:4, 6, 9, 15–16, 26–27

Gideon is a strong man who wants to kill wicked King Noah. Just as he is about to kill him, the Lamanite army attacks the city and the people run away. King Noah is killed and his son becomes king. What is his son's name?

_____

_____

_____

_____

Mosiah 20:21–22, 24–26

The king of the Lamanites comes to fight King Limhi and his people again. Limhi decides to make peace with the Lamanites. Limhi's people put down their weapons. Does it work?

_____

_____

_____

Mosiah 21:22–24

Remember when Mosiah sent Ammon and a group of men from Zarahemla to the city of Lehi-Nephi to check on the descendants of Zeniff? In this chapter, Ammon and his group arrive in Lehi-Nephi and meet Limhi, who is king. Limhi is Zeniff's grandson, and he is happy to find out that these travelers are from his grandfather's land. How happy does it say Limhi was?

_____

_____

_____

Mosiah 22:1–2, 13–14

Ammon helps Limhi and his people escape into the wilderness. They travel for many days and arrive in Zarahemla. What do you think it would be like to walk from one city to another for many days?

_____

_____

_____

_____

Mosiah 23:4–7

Remember Alma who believed the words of Abinadi, ran to the wilderness, and started preaching and baptizing? This chapter continues that story. Alma's people want him to be their king, but he says no. Why does he say no?

_____

_____

_____

_____

Mosiah 23:25, 36–37, 39

The Lamanite army comes to Alma's people in the city
of Helam. They take the city, and Amulon is made king.
The people of Alma become slaves to the Lamanites.
What does it mean to be a slave?

_____

_____

_____

_____

Mosiah 24:10–14

Amulon tells the people they can't pray. If the Lamanites
hear them praying, the people will be killed. What do
Alma's people do?

_____

_____

_____

_____

Mosiah 24:15–16, 19–20, 22, 25

How does the Lord help the people of Alma?

_____

_____

_____

_____

Mosiah 25:1–3, 17–18

Many Lamanites have chosen to join the Nephites. This shows that people can change. What do they ask Alma to do?

_____

_____

_____

_____

Mosiah 26:29–31

When we make mistakes, we can repent and Heavenly Father will forgive us. We also need to forgive others when they make mistakes. Have you ever forgiven someone? Write about it.

_____

_____

_____

_____

Mosiah 27:8, 11–12, 19

Mosiah's sons and Alma's son, whose name is also Alma, are all friends, but they are making some wrong choices. What happens?

_____

_____

_____

_____

Mosiah 27:22–24, 32, 35–36

Alma and the sons of Mosiah change after seeing the
angel. They try to fix their wrong choices by traveling
and preaching the gospel. Write about a time you made
a wrong choice. What did you do to fix it?

_____

_____

_____

_____

Mosiah 28:1, 6–7

The sons of Mosiah want to be missionaries. Do you
know people who were missionaries? Ask them to tell
you about their missions. Write down what you learn
from them.

_____

_____

_____

_____

Mosiah 29:1–2, 6, 11, 40

Mosiah convinces the people to have judges instead of one king. They love Mosiah because he helps them and is righteous. Whom in your life do you love? What do you love about them?

_____

_____

_____

_____

Alma 1:27–28

This is the record of Alma, the son of Alma. He is one of the young men who saw an angel. To "impart of their substance" means they shared their money and their things with others. Who do they share with?

_____

_____

_____

_____

Alma 2:1–4

What is Amlici like?

_____

_____

_____

_____

Alma 2:9–10, 14, 24, 28–31

Amlici's followers make him king and they start to fight the Nephites. What happens?

_____

_____

_____

_____

Alma 3:10–11

These verses say that it doesn't matter if a person is born a Nephite or a Lamanite. What matters is what they believe and if they choose to obey God's commandments. Heavenly Father sees our hearts. We should try to see other people the way Heavenly Father sees them. They are all His children. What is something you can do that will help you love everyone the way Heavenly Father loves them?

_____

_____

_____

_____

_____

_____

_____

Alma 4:6, 8–9

Pride means to think you are better or more deserving than someone else. In these verses, who starts having pride: members of the Church or people who are not members of the Church?

_____

_____

_____

_____

Alma 5:1, 14

Alma asks the members of the Church if they are trying to be like Christ. What is one way you can be like Christ?

_____

_____

_____

_____

Alma 6:5–6

Alma preaches to everyone, not just members of the Church. He also tells members of the Church to meet together often. Do you go to church often? Why does Heavenly Father want us to go to church?

_____

_____

_____

_____

Alma 7:23–24

This is a list that describes how we should be. List some positive qualities you like about people. Circle one of these qualities that you want to develop in yourself.

_____

_____

_____

_____

Alma 8:8, 11, 13–14, 16

The people in the city of Ammonihah make Alma leave their city. When Alma leaves, an angel appears to him. What does the angel tell Alma to do?

_____

_____

_____

_____

Alma 8:18–21, 23, 26–27, 30

Who is Amulek? What does he do for Alma?

_____

_____

_____

_____

Alma 9:30-33

Alma preaches to the people, but they don't like what he says. They try to grab him and put him in prison. What happens next?

_____

_____

_____

_____

Alma 10:7-11

This is Amulek's story about meeting Alma. He lists the blessings he has because he chose to obey the Lord. What are some of the blessings you have?

_____

_____

_____

_____

Alma 11:42-43

This is part of a speech Amulek gives to a man named Zeezrom. It is about what happens to our bodies when we die and then are resurrected. Our bodies will be perfect. What will your perfect body be like?

_____

_____

_____

_____

Alma 12:1, 7

Zeezrom is trying to argue with Amulek about the gospel. Alma starts to teach Zeezrom more. How does Zeezrom react?

_____

_____

_____

_____

Alma 13:28–29

Alma gives some advice. What does he say we should do?

_____

_____

_____

_____

Alma 14:1–4, 17, 23, 26–28

Alma and Amulek are put into prison. After a while, Alma prays and an amazing thing happens. What happens?

_____

_____

_____

_____

Alma 15:3–11

What happens to Zeezrom?

_____

_____

_____

_____

LLG

Alma 16:15–16

The people become righteous and the Lord gives them His Spirit. The Spirit is another name for the Holy Ghost. Have you ever felt the Holy Ghost? What did it feel like? How does the Holy Ghost help you?

_____

_____

_____

_____

Alma 17:1–3

These chapters are about the sons of Mosiah and their experiences. What does it say about the sons of Mosiah?

_____

_____

_____

_____

Alma 17:19–25

Ammon makes King Lamoni happy when he says he wants to live with King Lamoni's people. Ammon chooses to be one of the king's servants. What is his job?

_____

_____

_____

_____

Alma 17:26–28, 31–37

What does Ammon do to the men who scatter the king's flocks of sheep?

_____

_____

_____

_____

Alma 18:1, 8–10, 12, 14, 36, 40–43

Ammon is a faithful servant, which amazes the king. His example makes King Lamoni want to listen to the gospel. What happens after the king listens to Ammon preach?

_____

_____

_____

_____

Alma 19:1–2, 4–5, 8–12

The queen has great faith. What does Ammon tell her about the king?

_____

_____

_____

_____

Alma 20:2, 4, 8, 11, 26–27

Why does Lamoni's father decide to release Ammon's brothers from prison?

_____

_____

_____

_____

61

Alma 21:18–23

What does it mean to be "free"?

_____

_____

_____

_____

Alma 22:1–2, 13, 15–18, 21–23

Aaron is Ammon's brother. After being released from prison, he goes to teach the gospel to king Lamoni's father, who is also a king. What happens to the king? What other person had the same thing happen to him?

_____

_____

_____

_____

Alma 23:16–18

What is the new name for the believers?

_____

_____

_____

_____

Alma 24:1–2, 6–7, 12–13, 17–18, 24–26

The Amalekites and Lamanites are angry at the Anti-Nephi-Lehies and want to start a war with them. The Anti-Nephi-Lehies do not want to go to war. They say they would rather die than take the lives of any more people. They bury their weapons and promise never to use them again. How do the Amalekites and Lamanites react?

_____

_____

_____

_____

Alma 25:17

What are the names of the four sons of Mosiah?

_____

_____

_____

_____

Alma 26:1, 11–12

Ammon talks about how much joy he has. Why is he so happy? What makes you happy?

_____

_____

_____

_____

Alma 27:2, 5, 14, 21–22, 26–27

After some time passes, the Lamanites and Amalekites decide again to go to war with the Anti-Nephi-Lehies. Ammon takes the people of Anti-Nephi-Lehi and they travel to Zarahemla. There they are given land to make their new home. What does it say they were like?

_____

_____

_____

_____

Alma 29:1–2

This is Alma talking. What does he say his greatest wish is?

_____

_____

_____

_____

65

Alma 30:6, 43, 49–50, 52

Korihor is a man who tries to convince people that Jesus Christ isn't really going to come to earth and die for our sins. He makes fun of Alma and asks him to show him a sign that God is real. He is "struck dumb." What does that mean?

_____

_____

_____

Alma 31:8–10, 13, 22–23

The Zoramites do not pray every day, and they do not go to church. Instead, they stand on a tall tower one day a week, repeat the same words, and then go home. They never speak to Heavenly Father from their hearts in a personal way, the way Jesus taught us to pray. What is something you can do to make your prayers more personal and not say the same thing every time?

_____

_____

_____

Alma 32:1–3

Who does Alma and the other missionaries have success teaching? What do you think it means to be "poor in heart"?

_____

_____

_____

_____

Alma 33:2–8

LLG

In these verses, the word _cry_ means "pray." How does Heavenly Father answer your prayers?

_____

_____

_____

_____

Alma 34:17-28

Here Amulek talks more about prayer. Make a list of five things you can pray for.

_____

_____

_____

_____

Alma 35:3-6

The Zoramites don't like what Alma and Amulek teach. What happens to the people who believe?

_____

_____

_____

_____

Alma 36:1, 3

This is Alma speaking to his son Helaman. What will God do for those who trust Him?

_____

_____

_____

_____

Alma 37:1–4

Who does Alma give the plates to?

_____

_____

_____

_____

69

Alma 38:1–3

This is Alma speaking to his son Shiblon. Why does Alma have great joy for Shiblon?

_____

_____

_____

_____

Alma 39:1–2, 10

Alma tells his son Corianton to listen to his older brothers. Do you have an older brother or sister? If so, do they help you?

_____

_____

_____

_____

Alma 40:11–12

What do these verses say paradise is like?

_____

_____

_____

_____

Alma 41:14

Alma tells his son to "do good continually." What is one good thing you will do this week?

_____

_____

_____

_____

Alma 42:27

This verse is about agency. Heavenly Father wants to give us blessings, but He lets us choose between right and wrong. We are responsible for our choices. What does it mean to be responsible for your choices?

_____

_____

_____

_____

Alma 43:4, 9

What is important to the Nephites?

_____

_____

_____

_____

Alma 44:5–7

Zerahemnah is the leader of the Lamanite armies. Moroni is the leader of the Nephite armies. What does Moroni tell Zerahemnah?

_____

_____

_____

_____

Alma 45:2–8, 15

Alma blesses his sons. Helaman says he will keep the commandments with all his heart. What do you think that means?

_____

_____

_____

_____

Alma 46:3–4, 7, 11–13

The people start to leave the Church and follow Amalickiah. What does Moroni do?

_____

_____

_____

_____

Alma 47:1, 4

What does Amalickiah want?

_____

_____

_____

_____

Alma 48:1–3

Does Amalickiah get what he wants?

_____

_____

_____

_____

Alma 49:1–5

How do the Nephites protect their city?

_____

_____

_____

_____

Alma 50:12–14, 17–23

What is the promise the Lord gave Lehi that is being fulfilled?

_____

_____

_____

_____

Alma 51:22–27

Amalickiah is able to take over a lot of Nephite cities because Moroni is busy dealing with the fighting between his own people. Do you fight with your family members sometimes? Does it make your family stronger or weaker?

_____

_____

_____

_____

Alma 52:19–23, 27–29, 31–32, 37–38

Moroni and Teancum trick the Lamanite armies. What does Moroni ask the Lamanites to do?

Alma 53:10–14, 16–18, 20–21

Remember the people of Anti-Nephi-Lehi? They are also called the people of Ammon, because Ammon converted them to the Lord. They buried their weapons and promised to never fight. Their sons didn't make that promise. Their sons decide to fight for their families. We call them the stripling warriors. How many sons are there?

Alma 54:1–3, 16–18, 20

Ammoron became the leader of the Lamanites after Amalickiah died. Ammoron wants to trade his prisoners for Moroni's prisoners. Does Moroni want this too? In the letter Ammoron sends, what does he say he wants the Nephites to do?

Alma 55:1–2, 4–5, 8, 15–16, 21–24

Moroni decides to help his people escape from the Lamanites. Does his plan work?

Alma 56:1–5, 41, 43–49, 55–56

Helaman becomes the leader of the stripling warriors. They are strong and brave. Who taught them? What has your mother taught you?

_____

_____

_____

_____

Alma 57:6, 17–22

What else do these scriptures tell you about the stripling warriors?

_____

_____

_____

_____

Alma 58:38–41

Helaman finishes his letter to Moroni. In what city are Helaman and the stripling warriors?

_____

_____

_____

_____

Alma 59:1–2

How does Moroni react to Helaman's letter?

_____

_____

_____

_____

Alma 60:1–5

Moroni is upset that Pahoran, who is the leader over all the lands, didn't send help to him and his armies. Write about a time you were upset because things didn't happen the way you wanted them to.

_____

_____

_____

_____

Alma 61:1–3, 8–9

Pahoran couldn't help Moroni because he had his own problems. Is he mad at Moroni for complaining?

_____

_____

_____

_____

Alma 62:1–3, 6–8, 42, 48, 52

After Moroni helps make peace, what does it say about the people of Nephi?

_____

_____

_____

_____

Alma 63:1–3

Who has the plates after Helaman dies?

_____

_____

_____

_____

Alma 63:10–13

Helaman is named after his father. Where did your name come from?

_____

_____

_____

_____

Helaman 1:1–4

Pahoran's sons fight about who gets to be leader after their dad dies. Have you ever fought with a family member over something you both want? How did you fix it?

_____

_____

_____

_____

Helaman 3:20–21, 37

Helaman becomes their leader. He names his oldest son Nephi, just like Nephi who built a ship. Nephi followed "the ways of his father." How are you like your father or mother?

_____

_____

_____

_____

Helaman 4:1, 12–13

The Nephites lose almost everything. Why does that happen?

_____

_____

_____

_____

Helaman 6:14, 16–18, 37–39

The people are happy for a while, but they start to get greedy and steal from each other. What is the name of the group that causes so much trouble?

_____

_____

_____

_____

Helaman 7:10–14

Nephi prays in a tower. Do you know you can pray anywhere at any time? Where do you like to pray?

_____

_____

_____

_____

Helaman 8:1, 10, 26–28

The wicked judges try to take Nephi. Nephi tells them their leader has been killed by his brother. How does Nephi know that?

_____

_____

_____

_____

Helaman 9:1–4, 39–40

Is the chief judge really dead? Do people start to believe that Nephi really is a prophet?

_____

_____

_____

_____

Helaman 10:2–5

What does the Lord tell Nephi?

_____

_____

_____

_____

Helaman 11:1–10, 16–18

A famine is when there is not very much food. Why do you think Nephi prayed for something hard to happen to the people?

_____

_____

_____

_____

Helaman 12:1–5

The Lord blesses the people, but they forget to thank the Lord and become selfish. Life becomes hard until they become humble again. What can you do to remember to be thankful for your blessings?

_____

_____

_____

_____

Helaman 13:1–4

Why does Samuel get up on the wall to preach?

_____

_____

_____

_____

Helaman 14:1–6

Samuel is prophesying the birth of Christ. What is a sign of Christ's birth?

_____

_____

_____

_____

Helaman 15:1–5

Samuel tells the Nephites they need to repent. Right now, the Lamanites are more righteous than the Nephites. Samuel says the Lord chastens them because He loves them. *Chasten* means to correct or discipline. Is there someone who chastens you because they love you? How do they help you make better choices?

_____

_____

_____

_____

Helaman 16:1–3

How do the people react to Samuel's preaching?

_____

_____

_____

_____

3 Nephi 1:1–2, 15, 18–21

Remember the signs of Christ's birth? The people see all of those signs. Imagine the sun setting at night, but it stays light all through the night. What would you do if that happened?

_____

_____

_____

_____

3 Nephi 2:7–8, 11–13

How many years after the signs of Christ's birth did the wars start?

_____

_____

_____

_____

3 Nephi 3:1–3, 7, 11–15

The leader of the Gadianton robbers writes to the Lachoneus, the leader of the Nephites. What does he want? What does Lachoneus do?

_____

_____

_____

_____

3 Nephi 4:1, 5, 7–10, 20–21, 27

What do the Nephites do when they see the armies of Giddianhi, the leader of the robbers?

_____

_____

_____

_____

3 Nephi 5:1–3, 6

Do the Nephites believe the prophets?

_____

_____

_____

_____

3 Nephi 6:1, 4–5, 9–10, 12–14

The people are blessed, and then what happens?

_____

_____

_____

_____

3 Nephi 7:15–18, 26

Nephi's faith in the Lord is so great that he has angels with him every day and people believe him. What can you do to have faith like Nephi?

_____

_____

_____

_____

3 Nephi 8:3–10, 20–21, 23

The things happening are signs that Jesus died. How long is it dark?

_____

_____

_____

_____

3 Nephi 9:1, 15–18

Whose voice do they hear?

_____

_____

_____

_____

3 Nephi 10:1–6, 9–10

They hear Jesus's voice again. He says He protects them like a mother hen protects her chicks. When the darkness finally goes away, what do the people do?

_____

_____

_____

_____

3 Nephi 11:1–10

They hear another voice three times. What is it like? Who comes to them after they hear the voice?

_____

_____

_____

_____

3 Nephi 12:1

Jesus calls twelve Nephite Apostles and gives them the priesthood. We have twelve Apostles today. What are their names?

_____

_____

_____

_____

3 Nephi 13:1–4

Alms are things you give to people in need. We should do acts of service in secret, not brag about them or want people to see how nice we are. Have you ever done something kind for someone and not told it was you? Write about it. If you haven't, write your plan to secretly do something nice for someone this week.

_____

_____

_____

_____

3 Nephi 14:24-27

Do these verses sound familiar? There is a song about a wise man and a foolish man. Jesus says that if we listen to Him and do what He has asked of us, it is like we have built our houses on a rock instead of sand. When a storm comes, our houses will not fall down. This is a parable. The storm is a symbol of when hard things happen to us in life. Have you ever had a hard time? How did Heavenly Father and Jesus help you?

_____

_____

_____

_____

_____

_____

3 Nephi 15:21–24

After Jesus Christ was with the people in Jerusalem, He comes to visit the Nephites on the other side of the world. When He says "sheep" He means people. He loves all of God's children throughout the world. Do you think He knows you and loves you? How do you know?

_____

_____

_____

_____

3 Nephi 16:1–3

What does Jesus tell the Nephites?

_____

_____

_____

_____

3 Nephi 17:11–12, 19–24

Jesus blesses each of the little children. What happens next?

_____

_____

_____

_____

3 Nephi 18:1–6

LLG

This is called the sacrament. We use bread and water. How does taking the sacrament help you renew the promises you make when you are baptized?

_____

_____

_____

_____

3 Nephi 19:9-13

The people are baptized and receive the gift of the Holy Ghost. When it says "fire" it doesn't mean real fire. It could mean how they feel inside. Have you ever felt the Holy Ghost? When you pray, sing in Primary, or listen in church, how do you feel?

_____

_____

_____

_____

3 Nephi 20:1

Jesus tells the people to stop praying out loud but to continue praying in their hearts. What do you think it means to pray in your heart?

_____

_____

_____

_____

3 Nephi 22:7–10

Jesus is quoting the prophet Isaiah. He mentions Noah who built an ark. Do you know that story? How many of each animal did Noah bring on the ark?

_____

_____

_____

_____

3 Nephi 23:1–5, 11–13

Jesus says to pay attention to the words of the prophets. He also tells the people they need to write down their experiences. Do you have a personal journal you write in? Why do you think Heavenly Father wants us to write down our experiences?

_____

_____

_____

_____

3 Nephi 24:10–12

What is tithing? Why is it important? How does Heavenly Father bless us when we pay our tithing?

_____

_____

_____

_____

3 Nephi 26:13–17

What is one thing Jesus does when He is with the Nephites?

_____

_____

_____

_____

3 Nephi 27:1–3, 7

What is the name of Christ's church today?

_____

_____

_____

_____

3 Nephi 28:1–3

Jesus tells His disciples that they will live until they are seventy-two years old, and then they will come to live with Him. If you got to pick an age to go live with Jesus, how old would you be?

_____

_____

_____

_____

3 Nephi 30

What does Jesus say you should do?

_____

_____

_____

_____

4 Nephi 1:1–3, 19, 21, 24–26, 47–48

After Jesus Christ comes to the Nephites, they are righteous for many years. But then they start making wrong choices again. Nephi gives the plates to Amos, and Amos gives them to his son who was also named Amos. Who hides the plates?

_____

_____

_____

_____

Mormon 1:1–5

How old is Mormon when Ammaron tells him about the plates?

_____

_____

_____

_____

Mormon 2:1–3, 16–17

How old is Mormon when he becomes the leader of the Nephite armies?

_____

_____

_____

_____

Mormon 3:2-3, 8-9, 11

When the Nephites win the battle, they don't thank God. Instead, they brag about how good they are. What does Mormon do? Have you ever bragged about something you did or are good at? What is a better way to act when you accomplish something?

_____

_____

_____

_____

Mormon 4:16-19, 23

Who is winning, the Lamanites or the Nephites?

_____

_____

_____

_____

Mormon 5:1–2, 16–18

Why do you think Mormon decides to lead their armies again?

_____

_____

_____

_____

Mormon 6:1–2, 6, 10–11, 16–20

How does Mormon feel?

_____

_____

_____

_____

Mormon 8:1–6

Moroni has the plates and finishes the story for his father, Mormon. Moroni is the only righteous person left. He has no family. How do you think he is feeling?

_____

_____

_____

_____

Mormon 9:21–22, 30–31

Moroni is talking to us in our day. What is one thing he wants us to know?

_____

_____

_____

_____

Ether 1:1–2, 5, 33–35

During the time of King Mosiah, the people found some plates. This story is what was written on those plates. It is the history of a group of people called the Jaredites. It begins with a man named Jared and his brother. He is called the brother of Jared. If someone wrote about you but didn't use your name, what would they call you?

_____

_____

_____

_____

Ether 2:4–7

Where does the Lord want to lead them?

_____

_____

_____

_____

Ether 2:16–17

A barge is a kind of boat. What do the boats look like?

_____

_____

_____

_____

Ether 2:22–23

What problem does the brother of Jared ask the Lord to help him solve?

_____

_____

_____

_____

Ether 3:1, 4, 6, 11–14

The brother of Jared knows they need light in their boats to cross the ocean. He believes so strongly in the Lord's power that he sees Jesus's finger, and then Jesus shows Himself to him. Do you believe Jesus has all power and He will help you solve your problems? What is something hard for you that Jesus can help you with?

_____

_____

_____

_____

Ether 4:12

Where does good come from?

_____

_____

_____

_____

Ether 6:2–5, 9, 11–12

How many days do they travel in the boats?

_____

_____

_____

_____

Ether 6:13–15, 19, 22, 27–30

Who becomes king?

_____

_____

_____

_____

Ether 7:1–5, 7–9, 26–27

When Kib is king, he has a son who takes over the kingdom and puts him in prison. What is his name? His brother wins back the kingdom in a battle. He becomes a righteous king. What is his name?

_____

_____

_____

Ether 8:1–7

SO

The same thing happens to Shule's son Omer when he becomes king: his son Jared takes over the kingdom and puts Omer in prison. Jared's brothers battle him and take back the kingdom. Fighting with your family can cause a lot of problems. How does showing kindness and respect strengthen you and your family? What is something you can do to help your family argue less?

_____

_____

_____

Ether 9:28–31

What happens when the people ignore the prophets?

_____

_____

_____

_____

Ether 10:19–21, 28

Lib is a righteous king. What is it like for the people while he is their king?

_____

_____

_____

_____

Ether 11:15–18, 20–23

Do the people stay righteous?

_____

_____

_____

_____

Ether 12:1–5

Who is Ether? How long does it say he preached?

_____

_____

_____

_____

Ether 13:1–2, 13–14, 20–22

What do the people do to Ether?

_____

_____

_____

_____

Ether 14:19–20, 22, 31

What happens to the people?

_____

_____

_____

_____

Ether 15:12–13, 18–19

The people fight until they are all killed. Why don't they stop the wars?

_____

_____

_____

_____

Moroni 1

Moroni is done writing the story of the Jaredites. He is the last living Nephite and is hiding from the Lamanites. Why is he hiding?

_____

_____

_____

_____

Moroni 2—3

Moroni writes down some things he feels are important for people to know in the future. He talks about how to ordain priesthood members. The priesthood is the power and authority to do Heavenly Father's work here on earth. Why do you think Moroni writes about this?

_____

_____

_____

Moroni 4—5

Do these chapters seem familiar? Have you heard these words before? They are the prayers given at church when the sacrament is blessed. Next time you are at church, you can follow along with the prayer in your scriptures. What does Heavenly Father promise us if we always remember Jesus?

_____

_____

_____

Moroni 6:4-6

These verses are talking about going to church. What do you think being "nourished by the good word of God" means? What can you do at church to be "nourished"?

_____

_____

_____

_____

Moroni 7:1, 5, 13

People who help you make good choices are inspired by God. Have you ever helped someone else make a good choice?

_____

_____

_____

_____

Moroni 8:17, 22

Jesus Christ loves children. That's you! How do you feel knowing Jesus loves you?

_____

_____

_____

_____

Moroni 9:6

Mormon tells his son Moroni that even if other people are not being righteous, we still need to work hard to make good choices and teach others the gospel. Do you think this is hard sometimes? Do you think Heavenly Father will help you?

_____

_____

_____

_____

Moroni 10:3–5

This is called Moroni's promise. He says that when we are finished reading the Book of Mormon, we should think about what we have read. We should pray and ask Heavenly Father if the things we read are true. If we have faith and believe Heavenly Father will answer our prayer, the Holy Ghost will let us know it is true. Do you remember what the Holy Ghost feels like? How did you feel as you read the Book of Mormon? Will you pray and find out if it is true? Write down your experience reading and praying about the Book of Mormon.

_____

_____

_____

_____

_____

_____

_____